Jennifer Capriati

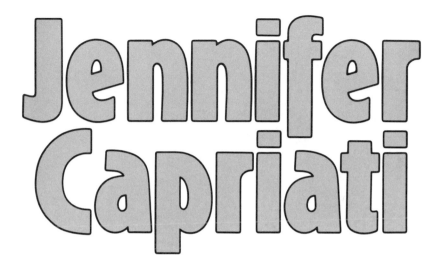

Jennifer Capriati

Tennis Sensation

Margaret J. Goldstein

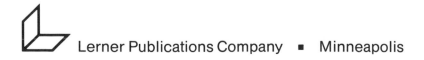

Lerner Publications Company ■ Minneapolis

To K.K.G.

This book is available in two bindings:
Library binding by Lerner Publications Company
Soft cover by First Avenue Editions
241 First Avenue North
Minneapolis, MN 55401

LIBRARY OF CONGRESS CATALOGING-IN-PUBLICATION DATA

Goldstein, Margaret J.
    Jennifer Capriati : tennis sensation / Margaret J. Gold-
stein.
        p.   cm. — (The Achievers)
    Summary: biography of professional tennis player Jen-
nifer Capriati
        ISBN 0-8225-0519-3 (library binding)
        ISBN 0-8225-9645-8 (paperback)
        1. Capriati, Jennifer—Juvenile literature. 2. Tennis players
—United States—Biography—Juvenile literature. I. Title.
II. Series.
GV994.C36G65   1993
796.342'092—dc20
[B]   92-38867
                                                                          CIP
                                                                           AC

Manufactured in the United States of America

1   2   3   4   5   6   98   97   96   95   94   93

Contents

Jennifer relishes a point scored in the gold-medal match.

Barcelona Bomber

Sixteen-year-old Jennifer Capriati was hot. She had been playing tennis for nearly two hours on a sticky summer day in Barcelona, Spain. The red clay of the tennis courts left a dusty red film on everything. The dust and heat choked Jennifer's lungs.

But Jennifer was excited too. She was in Barcelona trying to win a medal for the United States in the Summer Olympic Games. She wore a white tennis uniform with American flag patches on her skirt.

Jennifer had already beaten the hometown hero, Spain's Arantxa Sanchez Vicario, to reach the finals. Now, on August 7, 1992, there was only one person between Jennifer and an Olympic gold medal: the best female tennis player in the world, the 1988 Olympic gold medalist, Germany's Steffi Graf.

The powerful
Steffi Graf

Graf, 23, stood across the net and prepared to serve. The third set was tied four games to four. Jennifer was close to winning a fifth game—she led by three points. The first woman to win six games in the set would take the gold.

In their five previous matches, Jennifer had never beaten Steffi. She was determined to stop her this time. But Steffi Graf wasn't number one for nothing. She quickly picked up three points to tie the game.

If Jennifer could win two points, she'd have a chance to serve for the gold medal. She talked to herself and tried to pump herself up. The Olympic medal was so close that she could almost feel it hanging from her neck. But Jennifer just focused on Steffi's serve.

The next point ended after a long rally. Both players hit low, deep shots—back and forth across the net.

Finally, Jennifer put some extra force into a shot. Steffi couldn't return it. She hit the ball into the net.

Jennifer needed another point to win the fifth game. Steffi tossed the ball up in the air and hit a powerful serve. Jennifer was not intimidated. She hit a good return to Steffi's backhand, only to have the ball come rocketing back over the net. Jennifer gritted her teeth, brought her racket into position, and nailed a winner down the right side of the court.

Jennifer led five games to four. Now she would serve for the match and the gold medal. She slammed one good shot after another. Within minutes, Jennifer had scored four points. The gold medal was hers.

Jennifer was overjoyed. She blew a kiss to her parents, Denise and Stefano, who were cheering for her in the stands. "I'm so happy," she told TV announcer Bud Collins. "[The victory] means the whole world to me right now."

Later, a gold medal hung from a ribbon around Jennifer's neck. "I had the chills the whole time I was on the victory stand," Jennifer told reporters. "I've been here for two weeks, watching other American athletes receive their gold medals. I thought, 'That would be so cool to be up there.'"

"This is the first big win of Jennifer's career," said Marty Riessen, coach of the U.S. women's Olympic tennis team. "Nothing compares to this." Jennifer Capriati was the new Olympic champion.

Jennifer shows off her championship trophy after the U.S.
Open Juniors.

10

2

Junior Jam

The day before her first baby was born, Denise Capriati played tennis. Denise's husband, Stefano, sometimes worked at a country club, giving tennis lessons to members. Friends joked that Denise and Stefano's baby would be born holding a tennis racket.

On March 29, 1976, Jennifer Marie Capriati was born on Long Island, New York. Although Jennifer didn't hold a tennis racket in her hand, her athletic potential was clear from day one. Jennifer Capriati weighed an astounding 11 pounds at birth.

Denise and Stefano had come to Long Island from Spain for their daughter's birth (so that Jennifer would have American citizenship). Denise, originally from New York, was based in Spain as a flight attendant. Stefano, who was born in Italy, worked in Spain as a real estate marketer. Soon after Jennifer's birth, the Capriatis returned to Spain.

Denise and Stefano had high hopes for their daughter from the start.

"The day Jennifer was born, Stefano said he was going to make her a tennis player," Denise remembers. Stefano wasted no time in testing his daughter's athletic skills. When Jennifer was just three months old, Stefano put her through a routine of baby-style sit-ups. Next, Stefano threw his daughter into a swimming pool. She quickly learned to swim! At age two, Jennifer was competing against five-year-olds in local swim contests.

When Jennifer was four years old, the Capriatis left Spain and settled in Lauderhill, near Fort Lauderdale, Florida. Denise Capriati had missed living in the

United States, and she and Stefano wanted an American education for their children. The family now included Jennifer's one-year-old brother, Steven.

Stefano continued to work in real estate and teach tennis at a local country club. When Stefano gave lessons, Jennifer would scramble behind the automatic ball machine and chase the loose balls. Soon, she was swinging against the machine herself—hitting 100 balls without a miss.

Stefano knew his daughter had a special gift. He took four-year-old Jennifer to Holiday Park Resort in Fort Lauderdale to meet Jimmy Evert. Evert was a respected children's tennis coach. His daughter was Chris Evert, then America's greatest female tennis player. "I wanted her to start off with a wise man," Stefano said, "a guy who has already been through all of this [coaching Chris] and knows the psychology it takes to work with a little girl."

At first Evert refused to accept Jennifer as a student. He didn't coach children under age five, he explained. But when he saw Jennifer play, Evert made an exception.

"Stefano Capriati brought Jennifer around to see my father when she was about four years old," Chris Evert recalls. "Before too long she was beating all the other kids pretty badly. Then she graduated to the men club players and started beating them."

Although Chris was 22 years older than Jennifer,

people soon began to compare the two players—they both had a fierce two-handed backhand and a powerful baseline (backcourt) game. "When Jennifer was eight or nine, my dad told me that he hadn't seen anyone with so much talent since I started playing," Chris remembers.

Jimmy Evert coached Jennifer for seven years. Occasionally Jennifer and Chris practiced together, and they became close friends. "She's like a little sister or daughter to me," Chris says.

By 1986 few people doubted that Jennifer had a future in tennis. She dominated junior tournaments, beating girls far older and more experienced. In training, she preferred to play against boys; girls her own age weren't strong enough to return her powerful serves.

"I like to whip the boys," Jennifer said. "If it's a boy and I beat him, it feels good."

She switched coaches, leaving Jimmy Evert for Rick Macci, who worked with promising young tennis players at the Grenelefe Resort in Orlando, Florida. In 1987 the Capriatis moved to Orlando so Jennifer could work with Macci full-time.

Rick Macci recalls Jennifer's determination. In a practice session one day, a training partner smacked Jennifer in the forehead with a hard-hit drive. "Jennifer just put her head down for a second, wiped her eyes with her arm, came right back up, and got back into the ready position," Macci remembers.

People called Jennifer "the next Chris Evert." Evert plays here in the early 1980s.

"There were tears streaming down her face, but she refused to quit."

In the summer of 1988, Jennifer, at age 12, won two national 18s (tournaments for amateurs age 18 or under): the USTA (United States Tennis Association) Girls 18 Hard Court and Clay Court tournaments. She was the youngest winner ever in both events.

On the road to victory at the French Open Juniors

In 1989 Jennifer reached the quarterfinals (top eight players) at the Italian Open Juniors and Junior Wimbledon (the British national championship). She won the Belgian Indoor Juniors, the French Open Juniors, and the U.S. Open Juniors. She stood second on the International Tennis Federation's (ITF) 18-and-under amateur women's ranking. She was just 13 years old.

Although Rick Macci oversaw Jennifer's day-to-day training, Stefano Capriati served as head coach—setting the overall course for his daughter's career. Many people thought he pushed too hard. But Stefano was careful to encourage Jennifer without pressuring her. Some "tennis parents" only reward their child after a victory. Stefano took the opposite approach. He bought Jennifer a gift if she *lost* a tournament. Winning was a reward in itself, Stefano believed.

"When people first saw Stefano they said, 'Uh oh, another tennis parent,'" Chris Evert recalls. "But I see him as a very open person, and he wants Jennifer to experience other things in life besides tennis."

"I want her to have as much of a normal life as she can," Denise Capriati adds. "I'll never take her childhood away from her and Stefano won't either."

Even so, Jennifer found that leading an ordinary life wasn't easy for a tennis prodigy. She worked hard in public school in Orlando, maintaining an A average in her junior high classes. She enjoyed shopping, dancing, reading, and playing with her puppy, a Shih Tzu named Bianca. But she didn't have much time for close friendships. Tennis was the most important activity in Jennifer's life.

"If she went six hours on the court, she'd be ready for seven," Rick Macci remembers. "She's just a happy-go-lucky kid. But put a tennis racket in her hand and she turns killer...I'm telling you, she's scary."

By age 13, Jennifer was a celebrity.

Million-Dollar Debut

Late in 1988, Stefano Capriati had filed a petition with the Women's International Professional Tennis Council (WIPTC). Stefano asked that his daughter be allowed to play in professional tennis tournaments before her 14th birthday.

In 1986 the WIPTC had barred girls under age 14 from professional play. The ruling was made to protect teenagers from the injuries and pressures that often plague adult competitors.

Tennis prodigies Tracy Austin and Andrea Jaeger became professionals at age 15 and 14 respectively. Both women faded early in their pro careers, succumbing to injuries and stress. Steffi Graf, on the other hand, turned pro just four months past her 13th birthday. The early start hadn't put the brakes on Graf's swift climb to the top of women's tennis.

Jaeger (left) and Austin—shoot-
ing stars who fell early

"They made the age rule because of the burnout of just two players, Austin and Jaeger," Stefano argued. "But they don't know Jennifer. She's a very happy girl. She gets straight A's in school and she's very healthy. She just wants to improve."

The WIPTC had refused other players—including Yugoslavian Monica Seles—who wanted to turn pro before 14. But the council agreed to modify its rule slightly for Jennifer: she would be allowed to play professionally during the month of her 14th birthday.

Jennifer would make her pro debut at the Virginia Slims of Florida tournament on March 6, 1990—three weeks before she turned 14.

But Austin and Jaeger were quick to caution Jennifer about professional competition. They knew firsthand how much pressure the media places on young athletes —invading their privacy and often setting unrealistic expectations for success. "If she gets hurt, people will say she started too young," Jaeger said. "If she throws a racket or swears or loses a lot of first-round matches, they'll say the pressure has gotten to her."

"The most important thing for her is to enjoy tennis," Austin cautioned, "even when she starts losing. She's got to continue to develop her game and not be concerned with results. If she can, then the sky's the limit."

Jaeger and Austin's concerns were well founded. By early 1990, sportswriters were billing Jennifer as "the next Chris Evert." Tennis fans hungered for a new American star. Evert had retired, and Europeans like Graf, Seles, and Czechoslovakian-born Martina Navratilova now reigned in women's tennis.

"I think that everybody hopes so much that Jennifer is going to be the one, like Billie Jean [King] and myself," Chris Evert said. "It's like we [Americans] are starving for someone to come along and fill the void."

"She can definitely be the leading person in the '90s," added tennis veteran Pam Shriver. "The time is right to have a new star."

Sporting goods manufacturers were also searching for up-and-coming athletes to help sell their products. In Jennifer Capriati the sporting world saw not only a great tennis player but also a celebrity spokesperson.

Diadora, an Italian sportswear manufacturer, signed Jennifer to a $3-million, five-year advertising deal. Prince Manufacturing Company offered her $1 million over three years to promote its tennis rackets. Both companies promised Jennifer big bonuses if she performed well in tournaments.

So, before she had even entered her first pro tournament, Jennifer Capriati was a millionaire. She signed on with the International Management Group (IMG), a firm that handles business dealings for many of the world's greatest athletes. John Evert, Chris's brother, became Jennifer's business agent.

Life for the Capriatis revolved around Jennifer's career. Stefano gave up most of his real estate work and devoted himself to his daughter's training. Denise took a leave of absence from her job with Pan Am Airlines. The family left Grenelefe and moved to Saddlebrook, Florida (near Tampa), home of the Saddlebrook International Tennis Academy. There, Jennifer would train under Tom Gullikson and practice with pros Tommy Thompson and Richard Ashby.

"I've never seen anybody that good at this age," said Thompson. "She wants to be number one, not number two.

"If anything, she's overconfident, but that's what makes a champion. She doesn't worry if she can beat someone. For her it's a case of *when*, not *if*."

The publicity for Jennifer's professional debut began to mount in early 1990. The ABC television network shot a segment about Jennifer's life and training routine at Saddlebrook. NBC invited her to appear on the "Today" show. Sportswriters called Jennifer "the next great American tennis hope."

Denise, Jennifer, Steven, and Stefano stick together as a family.

Stefano discouraged Jennifer from reading about herself in magazines and newspapers. "I don't want her to feel the pressure to live up to what everyone is saying," Stefano said. "It's tough enough on adult players to read that stuff. It's too much for a 13-year-old."

"I don't know why everyone's going so crazy over me," Jennifer added. "I'm anxious to start my tennis career, but I feel like people are kind of expecting me to do something great right away."

Jennifer kept her calm as the tournament grew closer. She stayed confident. "Even though I'm going to be playing older ladies, when I'm out there playing, I'm as old as they are," she said. "I have no fear."

Finally, on March 6, 1990, Jennifer Capriati entered the Virginia Slims of Florida tournament in Boca Raton. Virginia Slims, a cigarette company, sponsors several professional tennis tournaments for women each year. The company awards prize money to the top finishers.

Like almost all pro tournaments, the Virginia Slims is an "elimination tournament." Entrants pair off against one another in the first round. Winners advance to the second round to face other first-round winners. With each round, half the field is eliminated. Finally, there are only two players left. They compete against each other for the tournament title.

Dozens of women, including some of the best tennis players in the world, had entered the Virginia Slims.

Many of Jennifer's friends came to root for her success at the Virginia Slims.

But Jennifer Capriati, the youngest of the contestants, received the most attention. "The tennis world is abuzz with anticipation," one sportswriter said.

Journalists begged Jennifer for interviews. More than 100 reporters swarmed around the Polo Club in

Boca Raton. Nearly 6,000 spectators turned out for the week-long event.

Chris Evert, unable to attend the tournament herself, sent Jennifer a telegram of encouragement. Jennifer's doubles partner, 46-year-old Billie Jean King, advised her on how to handle the pressures of competition.

Jennifer and the legendary Billie Jean King

Jennifer was excited—often too excited to sleep. She practiced privately to avoid the crowds. Sometimes she snuck off to Chris Evert's house, just a few blocks from the Polo Club, and watched TV. But unlike most of the contestants, Jennifer had to worry about more than the media, the fans, and the competition. She also had to do homework. She sent assignments back and forth to school by fax machine.

In her first match as a pro, Jennifer came out punching. Her serves were clocked at 94 miles per hour. Only the top women in tennis could hit the ball that fast!

Mary Lou Daniels, 28, was the first opponent to fall. In the following rounds, Jennifer picked off Claudia Porwik, Nathalie Tauziat, and Helena Sukova—ranked 10th in the world.

Jennifer had reached the semifinals; she was one of four players left in the tournament. She would face Laura Gildemeister in the semifinal match.

A tennis match is made up of points, games, and sets. The first player to score four points (with a lead of at least two points) wins the game. The first player to win six games (with a lead of at least two games) wins the set. In women's tournaments, the first player to win two sets wins the match.

If the score of a set reaches six games to five, the set continues. A score of 7-5 ends the set. A score of 6-6 leads to a special play-off game called a tiebreaker.

Both sets in Jennifer's semifinal match with Laura Gildemeister came down to tiebreakers. Jennifer bore down. "I like to fight," she said. "When I hear the crowd getting into it, I really get into it too." Jennifer won both tiebreakers to take the match.

Jennifer Capriati had reached the finals of her first professional tournament. There was only one other player to face—Argentina's Gabriela Sabatini, number three in the world. Jennifer's streak ended there, with Sabatini defeating her 6-4 in the first set and 7-5 in the second. But Sabatini was impressed by the talent of the young newcomer. "I had to play my best tennis to beat her," Gabriela said.

Only Sabatini could stop Capriati in Boca Raton.

Jennifer congratulates Gabriela on her win.

Fans, sportswriters, and sportswear companies were equally starstruck. Jennifer had lived up to her billing as the new golden girl of tennis. "This wasn't a debut," said one tennis commentator. "It was a premiere."

Companies like Oil of Olay thought Jennifer was a dynamic spokesperson for their products.

Net Worth

In April 1990, in her third professional tournament, 14-year-old Jennifer Capriati reached the finals of the Family Circle Magazine Cup held on Hilton Head Island, South Carolina. Along the way she had beaten fifth-ranked Arantxa Sanchez Vicario, 6-1, 6-1, before finally being stopped by tennis legend Martina Navratilova, 6-2, 6-4, in the final.

One of the prizes offered to the tournament winner was a Mazda Miata sports car. "It's just as well I won it," Martina said, "since Jennifer can't drive."

Not only was Jennifer still more than a year away from a driver's license, she had to contend with the demands of the eighth grade. The night before beating Sanchez Vicario, Jennifer worked on a history paper—which she faxed to her teacher at the Palmer Academy, a private school in Wesley Chapel, Florida.

But it was easy to forget that Jennifer Capriati was just a teenager. By the end of the 1990 season, Jennifer had earned nearly $300,000 in prize money. She had signed two new multimillion-dollar endorsement deals — with Oil of Olay, makers of skin-care products, and Texaco oil company. The Home Box Office network signed Jennifer to appear in a TV special called "The Building of a Champion."

Jennifer had played in 12 tournaments, compiling 42 wins and 11 losses. She had won a tournament, the Puerto Rico Open, and had reached the finals in two others. She had reached the semifinals of the French Open, becoming the youngest player ever to reach the semis in a "grand slam" event. (Wimbledon, the U.S. Open, the Australian Open, and the French Open are called grand slam tournaments.) She was ranked number eight in the world and number three in the United States. She was named the World Tennis Association's Most Impressive Newcomer.

Along the way she had some upsets and some disappointments. In the French Open, Jennifer clobbered Mary Joe Fernandez in the quarterfinals but then lost to 16-year-old Monica Seles in the semifinals. At Wimbledon Jennifer lost to Steffi Graf, 6-2, 6-4, in the fourth round.

But even Graf was a bit shaken after her victory. "It's strange. I don't feel old," Steffi said. "But this girl...she seems already great."

Jennifer was great. But she was still inexperienced. Many young tennis players surge to the top one year and fade the next. The occasional upset or tournament win does not turn a rookie into a champion.

Along with her early victories, Jennifer suffered many disappointments on the tennis court.

Jennifer had beaten many fine players in 1990. But she hadn't defeated any of the "Big Four" of women's tennis: Steffi Graf, Monica Seles, Gabriela Sabatini, and Martina Navratilova. But Jennifer would be patient. After all, she was only 14.

Going into 1991, tennis veteran Billie Jean King warned Jennifer about "sophomore slump." After the fanfare of the professional debut dies down, rookies often suffer in their second season. "Sophomore year is the dangerous one," King explained. "The first year, everything is new, and nobody really has the book [strategy] on you. But it gets tougher after that. The one thing I've stressed to Jennifer is to just keep the love of the game very close to her heart."

The tennis world had fallen in love with Jennifer Capriati in 1990, and Jennifer had returned the affection. She talked to the fans, smiled brightly for the cameras, and kidded with reporters. She was thrilled just to meet, let alone compete with, the greatest tennis players in the world.

But Jennifer's attitude began to change. "Last year, playing good matches and getting close was good enough," she said. "This year my goal is to forget about coming close and beat some of these top players. I don't just want good matches, I want to win."

But, as King had predicted, Jennifer's sophomore season started out rough. She lost to Helena Sukova at the Virginia Slims of Chicago, lost to Gabriela

Sabatini in the semifinals at the Virginia Slims of Florida, and lost to Monica Seles in the quarterfinals at the Lipton International Players Championship.

Jennifer's winning streak stopped when she came up against Monica Seles and the other "Big Four" champions.

To win, Jennifer would need more concentration and more privacy. "I can't be everything to everyone," she said. "[The fans and reporters] expect me to do all this stuff because I did it last year. But this year it's a little different. Sometimes I need to be by myself and just be able to go and watch a match privately without having to sign autographs or talk to anyone."

Tennis great Martina Navratilova was favored at Wimbledon.

Jennifer wasn't friendly to her opponents either. "On the tennis court I can't be nice," she said. "I say to myself, 'Come on, you don't want to lose. Fight back!'"

At Wimbledon in July, Jennifer fought her way into the quarterfinals. There, she came face to face with Martina Navratilova, 20 years older than Jennifer and the winner of nine Wimbledon titles. When the match was suspended midway through due to rain, Stefano tried to keep Jennifer calm. "Just go out and enjoy," he told his daughter. "Play. Have fun."

When the match resumed, Jennifer played her best tennis. She beat Navratilova, 6-4, 7-5. For the first time since 1977, Martina Navratilova would not be going to the semifinals at Wimbledon. Instead, Jennifer Capriati became the youngest Wimbledon semifinalist in history.

Although she lost in the semis to Sabatini, 6-4, 6-4, the quarterfinal victory at Wimbledon was a turning point for Jennifer. "Inside it made me believe I could be a top player," she said. "I just think it's more vivid, more clear to me now. It's still going to take a lot for me to get up there. [But] I see it down the road."

The road to the top was shorter than Jennifer realized. The Big Four had begun to fall. On August 4, 1991, Jennifer knocked off Monica Seles in the Mazda Classic in Carlsbad, California. She beat Seles again in a final-set tiebreaker to win the San Diego Open.

Then she beat Gabriela Sabatini for the first time to win the Canadian Open.

Jennifer was proud of her victories over the best players in the world. She was proud of her tournament wins. But one event meant more to Jennifer than any other: the U.S. Open.

"The U.S. Open is played in my country," she said. "I'm playing in front of my people, and I know they'll really be behind me. If you win the U.S. Open, you become a legend in the United States."

The 1991 U.S. Open turned out to be bittersweet for Jennifer. She beat Sabatini, the defending U.S. Open champion, in a stunning quarterfinal upset. "I have come close," she said. "Now I want to go all the way."

In the semifinals against Seles, Jennifer served twice for the match point but slipped up both times. She lost to Seles, 6-3, 3-6, 7-6. "Sometimes I can't sleep at night thinking about that match," Jennifer says, "just thinking that I was two points from the final of the U.S. Open. I'd give anything to go back to that moment and win."

In November, at the Virginia Slims of Philadelphia, Jennifer tried out some new equipment—contact lenses. She had applied for a Florida driver's license (15-year-olds can drive in Florida) and had failed the vision test. The new lenses helped Jennifer beat Sabatini in the semis, but she lost again to Seles in the finals.

Jennifer celebrates her quarterfinal upset at the U.S. Open.

When the 1991 season was over, Jennifer had collected more than $500,000 in prize money and more than $5 million in endorsement income. She ranked 26th on the *Forbes* magazine list of the world's highest paid athletes. Jennifer bought a BMW automobile for herself and a new house for her family.

She was ranked number six in the world. She had beaten Sabatini, Seles, and Navratilova. Only one Big-Four player was left to beat—Steffi Graf.

Powerhouse

At age 15, Jennifer Capriati wore size 10½ shoes. She stood 5 feet, 7 inches tall and weighed 135 pounds. She could hit a tennis ball at a speed of more than 100 miles per hour. Jennifer was bigger and stronger than most girls her age. She had a big appetite. And she was still growing.

Tennis experts marveled at Jennifer's powerful two-handed backhand, her rocketlike serve, and her precision ground stroking (hitting the ball after it bounces). "Jennifer's got the best ground strokes I've ever seen," Chris Evert said.

Jennifer had worked hard to become a world-class athlete. She endured grueling practice sessions, daily runs, and exhausting footwork drills. "You must be born with the proper body," Stefano points out. "But then you have to use that body properly."

Could a young teen-
ager hold up on the
grueling pro circuit?

Teen athletes face special problems, though. Ado-
lescents are not fully grown. Their bones and muscles
aren't as strong as those of adult competitors. Many
young tennis players, most notably Tracy Austin and
Andrea Jaeger, have suffered career-ending injuries
by pushing their bodies too hard too early.

Throughout Jennifer's childhood, many people
warned the Capriatis about problems that threaten
teen athletes. "[Jennifer is] capable of competing at
the highest level, but not capable of dealing with the

physical and emotional stress," warned sports psychologist Jim Loehr. "She needs to pick the right tournaments, mixing stress with relaxation."

Stefano wanted to protect his daughter from injury and stress. But he hadn't wanted to postpone her pro career. In 1989 Stefano had checked Jennifer into the Virginia Sportsmedicine Institute in Arlington. "We didn't go because she was sick," Stefano explained, "but because she was healthy."

After administering a series of tests, the staff of the institute put Jennifer on a special training program intended to increase her power and flexibility. The exercises were designed not only to improve Jennifer's tennis game but also to strengthen her body and help prevent injury.

Like Stefano, Jennifer's coaches were cautious in the early years. They didn't want to push the young player past her physical limits. In December 1991, Jennifer switched coaches again, leaving Tom Gullikson for Steffi Graf's coach, Pavel Slozil. Jennifer also signed on with physical trainer Pat Etcheberry.

Slozil and Etcheberry felt that at 15, Jennifer was ready for an adult training program. She began a new routine, including weight lifting for upper-body strength, two- to three-mile daily runs for endurance, and wind sprints for speed. The regimen was combined with three hours of tennis and a full day of high school. (On the road, Jennifer studies with a tutor.)

Jennifer plays with intensity and spirit.

Under Slozil, Jennifer sharpened her skills. She added more topspin to her serves and forehand shots, making them even harder to return. She improved her wrist control, which helps her place shots precisely where she wants them.

Jennifer plays best near the baseline, but wants to become better at net play. "I'm still not very comfortable at the net," she explains. "I don't think I'll ever really be a net person; I guess I was just born a baseliner. Still, I'm trying."

Tournament play has made Jennifer tougher mentally as well as physically. "As you go on, you get wiser," she explains. "To win against the top players, you've got to think a little more out there."

"Capriati is now a smarter player with a game that has more variety," notes retired American pro Stan Smith. "She can work a point better with an array of shots and spins instead of simply blasting away."

Jennifer doesn't give up. Everyone admires her energy and her fighting spirit. "You can't imagine how good she is," exclaims training partner Rick Ashby. "She improves incredibly quickly. She hits so hard, shows no mercy, runs like a racehorse."

"She's here to stay," says Monica Seles. "And she'll be a tough opponent for many, many years to come."

Gold Rush

As 1992 began, the tennis world was expecting wonders from Jennifer Capriati. During her first two professional seasons, she had beaten some of the best players in the world. She was poised for a grand slam win.

Tennis fans loved Jennifer. But some fans didn't like her parents. Many people accused Stefano and Denise Capriati of using their daughter's talent for their own financial gain. The Capriatis had pushed Jennifer too far too fast, people said. The critics predicted that Jennifer would crumble under the pressure.

"People have criticized us and said, 'Oh, she's so young,'" Denise Capriati answered. "[But] she's doing a really good job of balancing her own life. She loves tennis and she's willing to sacrifice as much as she has to. But she also loves school and her friends, and she's trying to do it all."

"She is a happy girl with a happy life," Stefano added. "She's an honor student, with a lot of friends …and she loves the game. That has nothing to do with the parents."

Through all the controversy and publicity, Jennifer seemed undisturbed. "I think the media is a little out of control," she once remarked. "I'm just a kid, and I have this talent, and I don't know why everyone is going just crazy over it."

In February 1992, however, a scowl spread across Jennifer's normally happy face. After a disappointing series of matches in Australia and Asia, Jennifer—overweight and frustrated—had a fight with her father, canceled an exhibition match, and flew home to Florida. "[Tennis is] becoming too serious," she complained.

The media quickly jumped on the story. Tabloid newspapers said that Jennifer's tennis career was through. Sportswriters said she was fat. They pointed to her taste for black nail polish, skull rings, and heavy metal groups like Metallica and Guns N' Roses and declared her a teenage rebel.

Was Jennifer burning out? Were the predictions of Austin, Jaeger, and numerous sports psychologists coming true? Or was Jennifer just a normal teenager who needed some privacy and some freedom?

Stefano quickly took action. He stepped aside as Jennifer's head coach and left the job entirely to Pavel Slozil. "Right now she needs me as a father, not as a coach," he announced. "This way we can keep them separate."

"Jennifer is not a burnout," insisted Slozil. "But she has to find the right motivation again...Tennis is Jennifer's fun and her hobby and her business. She needs time for herself."

Jennifer agreed. "I'm dealing with tennis," she explained. "Plus you've got the added pressure of trying to be accepted by your friends, dealing with math and chemistry teachers, and dealing with rules at home. I mean, it's a lot."

Many people thought Stefano pushed his daughter too hard.

But Jennifer's biggest complaint was that the media had blown her problems out of proportion. "Everyone has arguments with their parents," she said. She was, in many ways, an ordinary teenager.

But she was also a millionaire with a full-time job on the tennis court. She could easily have dropped out of school and eliminated the stress caused by tests and homework. But Jennifer *wanted* to go to school. She wanted to be a regular high school student. She was tired of being "America's tennis sweetheart."

"If I like black fingernails, I'm going to do it," she said. "If I like to dress in tie-dye, what's the problem? ...I'm not the next Chris Evert. I'm different. I'm me."

Jennifer decided to take a six-week break from tennis. She cut junk food from her diet and shed the extra pounds that had slowed her down early in the year. She dismissed Coach Slozil—choosing to train independently for a while and to take more control of her own career.

The well-needed rest renewed Jennifer's commitment to her sport. There were many big tournaments on her schedule in 1992. But one event was more important than the rest—the Olympics.

In late July, Jennifer traveled to Barcelona, Spain, with the United States Olympic tennis team. Jennifer's long-time rivals Steffi Graf and Arantxa Sanchez Vicario would be among many competitors representing their countries at the 1992 Games.

Arantxa Sanchez Vicario would be a threat in Barcelona.

But three of the world's top five women—Monica Seles, Gabriela Sabatini, and Martina Navratilova—wouldn't be in Barcelona. All three wanted to play at the Games. But the International Tennis Federation had set strict rules about who could enter. To make the Olympic team, a player had to have represented her nation in the Federation Cup the year before.

Steffi Graf, the one superstar Jennifer had never beaten

Seles, Sabatini, and Navratilova had all missed the tournament.

Many would argue that a tennis tournament without Seles, Sabatini, and Navratilova wasn't much of a contest. But Jennifer didn't mind. Steffi Graf *would* be competing. Jennifer had beaten all the other top players. But she had never beaten Steffi Graf.

On August 7, 1992—after putting away Sanchez Vicario in the semis—Jennifer finally bested Steffi Graf. "It was one of my greatest matches in terms of fighting for everything, running down balls, not giving up when things weren't going my way," she said after the gold-medal victory. "I was really patient the whole tournament. But I was also aggressive."

Not only did the victory prove that Jennifer was out of her early-year slump, it also launched her to new heights. "It built up my confidence," Jennifer explained. "Steffi was always the one I couldn't beat. Now I feel I've passed a certain level....It kind of proves to everybody—most of all it proves to me— that I can win a big title."

As excited as Jennifer was to beat Steffi Graf, she was even more excited about the Olympics. She liked living in the Olympic Village and meeting athletes from other countries. She was proud to win a medal for the United States. Jennifer cried with happiness when she stood on the victory stand and heard "The Star-Spangled Banner" played in her honor.

Jennifer Capriati has high expectations for the future. She wants to win a grand slam tournament—especially the U.S. Open. She wants to be number one.

"I'm going to be very confident," she said after the Olympics. "I know I can beat all the top players." No one can slow down Jennifer now.

Opposite: The Olympic champion celebrates her victory.

Steven gives his sister a big hug.

ACKNOWLEDGMENTS

All photographs used with permission of Carol L. Newsom except pp. 2, 6, Clive Brunskill/Bob Thomas Sports Photography; p. 55, Bob Thomas Sports Photography.